International prize for urbanism
Lee Kuan Yew World City Prize, 2016

The city with the best perception of quality of life among its inhabitants
Cómo Vamos Network of Cities (Colombia), 2015

The city with the highest score in the "Global survey regarding the state of Smart Cities"
Indra (Spanish consulting and technology company), 2014

Innovative City of the Year
Citigroup, Wall Street Journal and Urban Land Institute, 2013

Sustainable Transport Award
Institute for Transportation and Development Policy, 2012

The term *guayacán* derives from the Taíno word *waiacan* and refers to trees with colorful, explosive and more or less simultaneous blooming seasons. In the Aburrá Valley those with yellow blooms are the most common, but there are pink, white and lilac-blooming varieties as well. The first *guayacanes* were planted in the El Poblado area during the second half of the nineteenth century and in the Prado neighborhood in the 1930s. Today it is common to see them throughout the metropolitan area.

Unpredictably, they shed their usual green leaves twice a year on average, after two rainy and two dry periods. Then they bloom with an abundance of flowers that will be gone in a week's time after carpeting the ground with their petals and creating a short-lived but memorable romantic tableau.

The Integrated Transportation System of the Aburrá Valley (SITVA) is made up of Metro trains, Metrocable cable cars, Metroplús articulated buses, and streetcars. The Metro serves as an axis that runs through the city from north to south and extends to the neighboring municipalities of Bello, Envigado, Itagüí, Sabaneta, and La Estrella. The streetcars, Metrocable gondolas, Metroplús buses, and transfer routes branch out from the Metro stations to various points in the east and west of the city.

This is the largest public transportation system in the country and a relevant model in Latin America. In 2012 the Institute for Transportation and Development Policy awarded Medellín the Sustainable Transport Award. It is hoped that the improvement and expansion of this system will discourage the use of private transportation and ease traffic congestion.

The tradition of the *bandeja paisa* (*Paisa* platter) in Antioquia and other territories of Colombia dates back to the times of the Antioquean colonization (18th and 19th centuries) when muleteers carried the *envuelto antioqueño* (Antioquean wrap) as their road rations, bundled in a banana leaf. It was a composition rich in carbohydrates to provide energy for long hard days as they trekked rough trails, herding mule trains to the next village, resting until dawn, and continuing their journeys that could last up to two weeks. Nowadays the *bandeja paisa* is common on menus in major cities throughout Colombia. Its main ingredients are rice, dry ground beef, *chicharrón* (pork rinds), fried egg, slice of ripe plantain, chorizo, *arepa* (corn griddle cake), *cargamanto* beans, tomato and onion stew, salad and avocado. Since it is such a rich and abundant meal, it is served on a platter rather than a regular plate.

Juan Carlos, a typical mango vendor

Fruit vendors are a common sight downtown, on the main streets and avenues, in sports areas, in neighborhoods and near schools and universities. Green mangos (see photo) are traditionally eaten with lemon and salt, a sour combination that may cause an involuntary one-eyed wince.

Potatoes are grown in rural areas of Antioquia. This treasure of the Andes saved Europe from famine in the seventeenth century and today is a foodstuff for billions of people on all continents. In Medellín it is common to find stands selling fresh hot potato chips on the streets.

Wooden relic of
Jesus of Nazareth

Rosary beads

The Catholic faith is the traditional spiritual doctrine in Colombia; Catholicism influenced the founding of cities and towns since the times of the Spanish Conquest. The Archdiocese of Medellín has more than three hundred and thirty parishes ministering to the faithful throughout the Aburrá Valley. The Virgin of the Candelaria is the patron saint of the city; the first parish in the colonial village of Medellín was established in her honor. There is also abundant veneration of the Sacred Heart of Jesus, Our Lady of Mt. Carmel, and Mary Helper of Christians.

From left to right: Religious cards of Our Lady of Mount Carmel, the Sacred Heart of Jesus and Mary Helper of the Christians

The *carriel* was the satchel par excellence of the muleteers who settled the *paisa* areas of Antioquia. There are various explanations of the origin and use of the term *carriel*. Some say that it evolved from the English term "carry-all", the Spanish "guarniel", or the French "carnier" (hunter's bag). Nowadays, you rarely see anyone carrying this accessory in the streets of Medellín, although it is still seen in the rural *paisa* towns of Antioquia and the Eje Cafetero (Coffee Region). During the *Feria de la Antioqueñidad* (Antioquean Heritage Festival) celebrated every year in elementary schools, children wear—possibly for the only time in their lives—a traditional Antioquean outfit, which includes a *carriel*. Perhaps that is why every Antioquean knows that the *carriel* is a symbol that represents them, although they may never use it themselves.

Silleteros are peasants from the village of Santa Elena in the mountains east of Medellín. Until the mid-twentieth century they used to trudge from their farms down steep, narrow dirt roads to the city, transporting flowers and vegetables in wooden frames called *silletas* that they carried on their shoulders. To celebrate this unique feature of the city, the Parade of *Silleteros* was first organized as a cultural display in 1957, and the Feria de las Flores (Festival of Flowers) was established. Nowadays, nearly five hundred *silleteros* participate in this two-and-a-half kilometer parade, carrying *silletas* with elaborate figures made of flowers and weighing from sixty to ninety kilograms. The parade and festival are held every year in August. The *silleteros* of Santa Elena have been declared a Cultural Heritage of the Nation by the Congress of Colombia.

A monumental *silleta* under the
equatorial sun of Medellín

Scents of incense, rosewood and other medicinal and aromatic herbs; necklaces and earrings made by hand; fabrics and wood crafts; antiques and oddities of all kinds; and all those things that supposedly nobody would ever sell or buy, are available in the Mercado de Sanalejo, the city's premier flea market, which has taken place every first Saturday of the month since 1974 at the Parque de Bolívar in downtown Medellín, from 8 a.m. to 6 p.m.

Collectible dolls await a buyer in the Mercado de Sanalejo

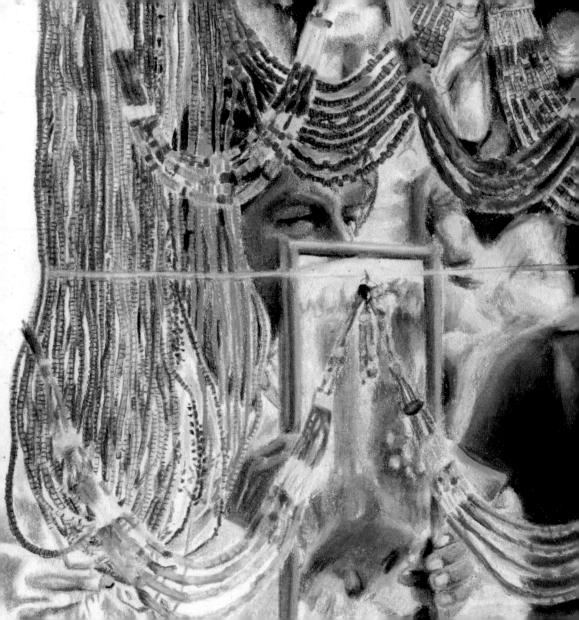

The dance team of Adelaida Mejía and Jhon Alexánder Blandón in a typical bar in downtown Medellín

In Medellín the tango is still heard, composed, performed, and danced more than a century after it emerged seven thousand kilometers away in the cities of Buenos Aires (Argentina) and Montevideo (Uruguay). Apparently the fascination with the tango in the capital of Antioquia derives from the fact that in 1935 the greatest and most famous tango singer of all times, Carlos Gardel, died in this city, the victim of a plane crash. According to researchers, although the public was already fond of tango, after his death they reaffirmed their taste for this music.

In downtown Medellín, the neighborhoods of Manrique and Barrio Antioquia, and the neighboring cities of Bello and Envigado, there are traditional bars where people drink aguardiente, beer, or black coffee while listening to tangos that may have been recorded around the first half of the twentieth century. There are also dance academies and troupes—some internationally recognized—that include performers of all ages, from children to senior citizens. Certain monumental spaces such as the Museo Casa Gardeliana (Gardel House Museum) and Plaza Gardel preserve the history of the tango. The International Tango Festival is held every year around June 24th, when Gardel's death is commemorated.

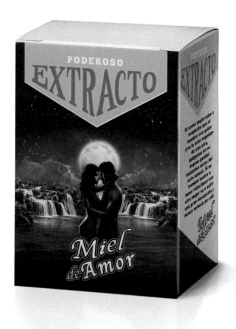

Amansa Guapos (Hunk Tamer), *Suerte Rápida* (Quick Luck), *Lluvia de Oro* (Shower of Gold) and *Miel de Amor* (Love Syrup). These are some of the potions that can be purchased at the esoteric shops in downtown Medellín. Essences and body washes to guarantee good fortune and success in love.

Explora Park is a collection of educational science and technology exhibits and events, including museums, shows, conferences and a planetarium. The interactive rooms offer activities regarding communication, physics and neuroscience. The planetarium presents astronomy shows and live trips to the edges of the known universe. The aquarium and

vivarium house hundreds of animal species from the rivers, seas, forests and jungles of Colombia. One of its most distinctive programs is *Ciencia en Bicicleta* (Science on a Bike), a series of lectures by experts from local researchers to Nobel Prize winners, intended to make scientific and technological knowledge available to average citizens.

The Orquideorama (orchid showroom), located inside the Joaquín Antonio Uribe Botanical Garden, is notable for its unique roof made up of hexagonal figures that resemble the union of large petals or beehives. It received the *Lápiz de Acero* award in Colombia for its architectural design, and special recognition from the Colombian Society of Architects. The Ministry of Housing of Spain awarded it the Best Architectural Work prize at the *VI Bienal Iberoamericana de Arquitectura y Urbanismo* (VI Biennial Spanish-American Architecture and Urban Design Show) in Lisbon, Portugal.

The Junín pedestrian promenade connects the needle-peaked Coltejer building with Parque Bolívar two blocks away. In the 50s, 60s, and 70s it was the hub of luxury, fashion, and entertainment for the high society of Antioquia. You can still visit most of the indoor shopping areas and some of the coffee shops and restaurants where the most distinguished residents of the city used to gather. They continue to be preferred meeting places for nostalgic people who recall the old days fondly.

In the Minorista marketplace you can purchase fruits, vegetables, legumes, breads, meats, fish, dairy, eggs, liquor, and new and used clothing; as well as traditional prepared dishes such as blood sausage, *empanadas* and *pasteles* (turnovers), stuffed potatoes, breaded dried fish, liver and onions, tripe soup, *sancocho* (stew), beans with pork rinds, and *bandeja paisa*, all of these at low prices. The warm aromas of frying food, vegetable soup, Colombian coffee, *aguapanela* (tea made from unprocessed brown sugar), and a hundred distilled herbs, blend with the colder odors of tropical juices, onions, potatoes, arracachas, and carcass meat. The soundtrack is popular music and raucous *carrilera* music that spills out of the saloons where heat and thirst are quenched with cold beer. In the background, one hears the employees of the various shops and stores address each other not by first names but by nicknames such as *mono* (blond), *primo* (cousin), *orejón* (big ears), or *pati-ancho* (bigfoot).

Israel Heredia and Cuadro Flamenco perform in the Otraparte House Museum

The Otraparte House Museum is the house where the philosopher and author Fernando González (1895-1964) lived his last years. He is considered by the Congress of the Republic of Colombia to be one of the most important Colombian thinkers of all time. His work exerted an important influence on Nadaísmo (a philosophical and literary movement that emerged in Antioquia in the 1960s). Currently this house is the headquarters of the Otraparte Corporation, dedicated to spreading Gonzalez's legacy and facilitating the expression of cultural alternatives.

The San Pedro Cemetery Museum was established in 1842 as the first private cemetery in Medellín, which at that point was still a small town. A number of people who were important national figures during the 19th and 20th centuries are buried there. This place is unique in the city. Besides guided thematic tours, it offers activities that encourage people of all ages to use it as recreational and cultural space. Events that take place regularly at the cemetery include *Me Muero por Jugar* (I'm Dying to Play), *Noches de Luna Llena* (Full Moon Nights) and *Vive el Cuento* (Live the Story). The idea, in part, is to try to demystify the dark image we have of cemeteries at night. Once a month, at 5:45 p.m., the event *Atardeceres en el Cementerio* (Sunsets in the Cemetery) is held. Visitors tour the galleries and admire the tombs and mausoleums while enjoying artistic performances amidst the magic that encompasses this world of graves.

Twilight at the San Pedro
Cemetery Museum

On Sundays and holidays more than 31 kilometers of local roadways are made available by the city for jogging, cycling and skating. Motor vehicles are banned on *Avenida del Río*, *Avenida El Poblado*, *Avenida Oriental* and the areas surrounding the Atanasio Girardot soccer stadium so that athletes can ride or jog safely.

Cycle path on *Avenida El Poblado*, under the "Green Tunnel" that reduces road heat between Medellín and Envigado

Near Parque Berrío, in the heart of Medellín, we find the Plaza de las Esculturas (Sculpture Plaza, also known as Plaza Botero), where more than twenty statues by famed local artist Fernando Botero are on exhibit. This plaza is the front yard of the Antioquia Museum, which is the temple of fine arts in the city, par excellence.

What appears to be a Caribbean shoreline is actually 1925 meters (6315 feet) above sea level. A two-hour drive from Medellín into the eastern area of Antioquia brings us to the spectacular Peñol-Guatapé reservoir. After the dam was built in 1972, the original town of El Peñol was flooded and now lies deep in the water. Guatapé has become a center for water sports, boats, and jet skis. Next to the reservoir is the Piedra del Peñol, also known as the Peñón de Guatapé, a 220-meter-tall monolith. It is a long climb up the 740-tread staircase, but from its top you will have a majestic view of the entire reservoir and the surrounding landscape that is worth every step.

View of the Peñol-Guatapé dam from the top of the rock

The Prado district is the only architectural heritage conservation area in the city. In the beginning (about 1926) it was a residential area for the upper class, with luxurious European style houses adapted to the local climate. Over time, the initial inhabitants moved to other parts of the city, leaving behind the glamour of those nostalgic mansions. Today it is common to find in Prado offices of NGOs, clinics, and homes for the elderly; but also artists, musicians, romantics, and playwrights; art galleries, theaters, fashion houses, craft workshops, coffee shops, and private gourmet kitchens; all converge in its retro atmosphere. Like a bubble, each estate is a house of mystery. You can find a magical underworld behind their façades, some threadbare, others enameled regularly to overcome old age.

The Águila Descalza theater, founded by the comedy troupe of the same name, is the most popular artistic and cultural institution in Prado neighborhood. The contemporary art center Casa Tres Patios, the Adrissa fashion house, and the Plazarte cultural center are also worthy of a visit.

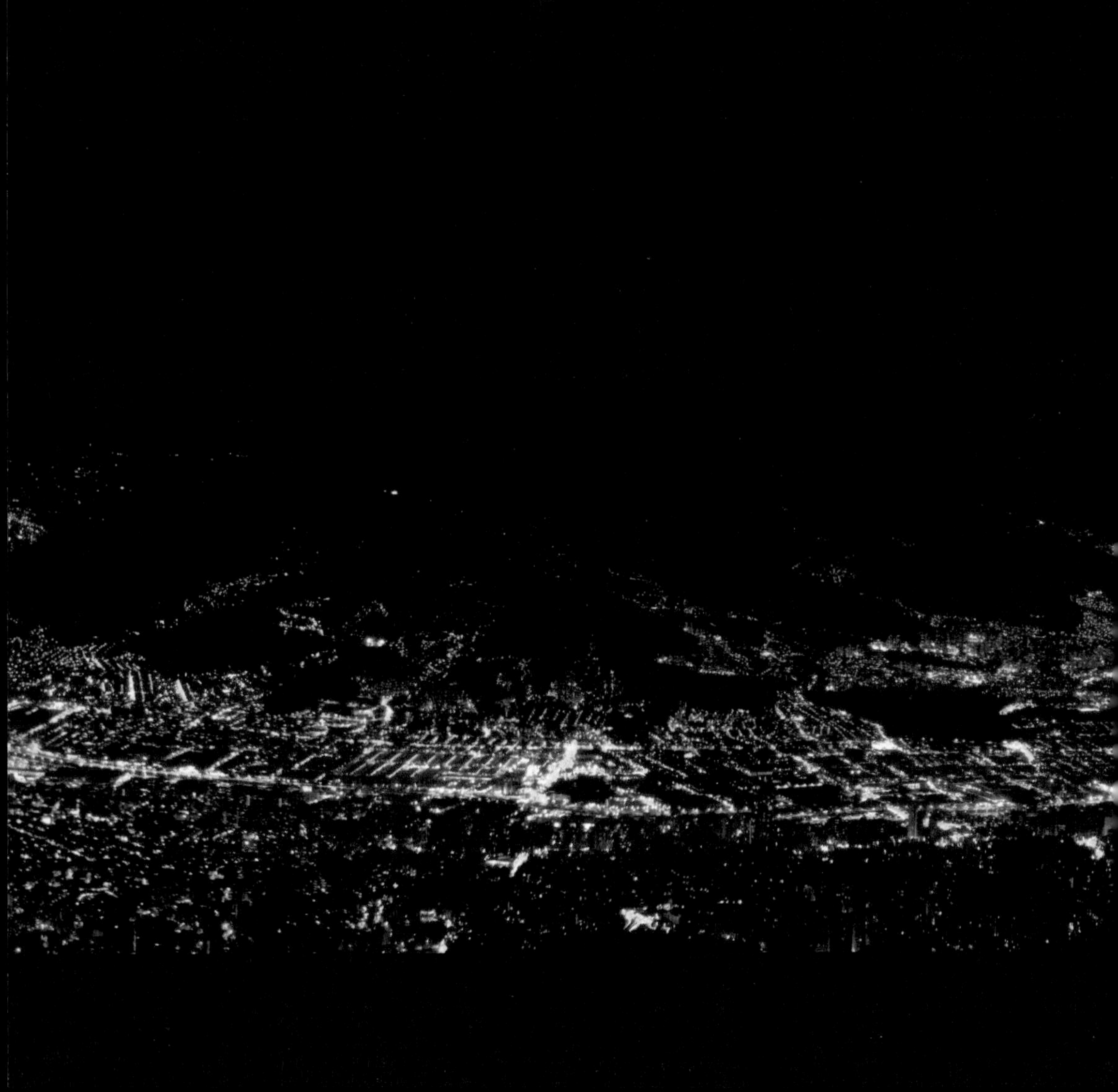

Oh, my beloved Medellín, city that I love,

where I have suffered, where I slowly die!

My thoughts have grown tragic amid your tall mountains,

the chaste gloom of your parks, your mad drive for money.

But I love your skies, clear and blue as a gringa's eyes.

(Fragment of the poem *Medellín, a solas contigo—Medellín, alone with you—*
by poet Gonzalo Arango)

Aburrá Valley seen from Avenida Las Palmas in Envigado

Aimdigital.com.ar. (2016). *El tesoro de Los Andes salvó del hambre a Europa.* **[Online] available at: http://www.aimdigital.com.ar.**
Newspaper article on potato cultivation in Europe. In the seventeenth century the consumption of potatoes increased on the European continent due to poor cereal harvests caused by the Thirty Years' War.

Arango, G. (2016). *Obra negra.* **Editorial Universidad Eafit. Medellín, p. 159.**
A work published in Buenos Aires, Argentina in 1974. The third edition is under way at Eafit University Publishers and features the compiling of Jotamario Arbeláez, who was a personal friend to the author and was part of the *Nadaísta* movement in the second half of the twentieth century.

Botanicomedellin.org. (2016). *Jardín Botánico de Medellín Joaquín Antonio Uribe // Medellín – Colombia.* **[Online] available at: http://www.botanicomedellin.org.**
Official site of Medellín's Joaquín Antonio Uribe Botanical Garden. The space is managed by nonprofit private organizations. The nature area was consolidated as of April 19, 1972, during the VII World Orchid Conference. The Flora Pavilion is part of the National Environmental System (Sina).

Epm.com.co. (2016). *Embalse Peñol Guatapé.* **[Online] available at: http://www. epm.com.co/site/comunidadymedioambiente.**
Informational website for the Peñol-Guatapé Reservoir, providing data regarding the capacity, supply and demand of the electricity generated by the reservoir, as well as information about events in the town of Guatapé.

Elpenol-antioquia.gov.co. (2016). *Sitio web del municipio El Peñol en Antioquia.*

[Online] available at: http://www.elpenol-antioquia.gov.co.
Official website of El Peñol city hall. The town is 62 kilometers far from the city of Medellín. The website provides tourism information including a guide to local tourist sites, festivals, hotels and restaurants.

Fao.org. (2008). *Año Internacional de la Papa.* [Online] available at: http://www.fao.org/potato-2008.
Official website of the International Year of the Potato in 2008, with the purpose of informing and raising awareness of the importance of this tuber as a strategic food for developing countries. Research and the improvement of production are also promoted to meet the goals set by the United Nations.

González Toro, R. (2015). *En Medellín se quedaron para siempre las voces del tango - Medellín - El Tiempo.* [Online] available at: http://www.eltiempo.com/colombia/medellin/la-historia-del-tango-en-medellin.
Newspaper article outlining the influence of tango on all social groups in Medellín, emphasizing the link between the Buenos Aires *lunfardo* dialect and the popular speech of Medellín natives, thanks to the connection of the inhabitants of the Antioquean capital with the lyrics and the musical expression of tango.

Guatape-antioquia.gov.co. (2016). *Sitio web del municipio Guatapé en Antioquia.* [Online] available at: http://www.guatape-antioquia.gov.co.
Official website of the Guatapé city hall. The town is located 75 kilometers from the city of Medellín. The website provides tourism information including a guide to local tourist sites, festivals, hotels and restaurants.

Inder.gov.co. (2016). *INDER Alcaldía de Medellín.* **[Online] available at: http://
www.inder.gov.co.**
Website of the Municipality of Medellín with access to the schedule of facilities
and programs for sport and recreational activities in the city. The Institute of
Sports and Recreation of Medellín (Inder) promotes physical activity and sports
as well as spaces for equity and harmonious coexistence.

Jaramillo Panesso, J. (1998). *Vení leéme.* **Universidad Autónoma Latinoamericana.
Medellín, pp. 65-68.**
A literary essay with references to historical information and texts on the history
and use of the *carriel* in Antioquia is included in this book. The author suggests
that in earlier times this accessory was called *guarniel* (a term included in the
dictionary of the Royal Spanish Language Academy). He quotes the *Diccionario
folclórico antioqueño* (Folkloric Dictionary of Antioquia) by Jaime Sierra García
to explain the origin of the word *carriel*.

Parqueexplora.org. (2016). *Parque Explora Medellín.* **[Online] available at:
http://www.parqueexplora.org.**
Official website of Parque Explora, an interactive park designed to awaken public
interest in science, art and technology.

Silleteros.com. (2016). *Sitio oficial de los Silleteros de Santa Elena.* **[Online]
available at: http://www.silleteros.com.**
Website of the Corporación de Silleteros de Santa Elena, providing information on
the history and culture of the *silleteros*, as well as news and activities of interest
to the community of Santa Elena.

Telemedellín (2015). *Tango Medellín.* **[Video] available at: https://vimeo.com.**
This documentary won the Simón Bolívar prize for best cultural broadcast in Colombia for its history of tango in Medellín. It presents testimony from representative characters as it tours the centers of bohemian life in the city where the tango can be heard, such as Salón Málaga, La Payanca, Homero Manzi, Patio del Tango and Casa Gardeliana, among others.

Vitullo, M. (2015). *El tango en Colombia: entrada al país a principios del siglo XX y permanencia en la región del Eje Cafetero luego de 1930...* **1st ed. [ebook] Buenos Aires: Universidad de Buenos Aires. Available at: http://jornadasdesociologia2015.sociales.uba.ar.**
Paper presented at the Sociology Conference held at the University of Buenos Aires in 2015. The author analyzes the spread of this popular Argentinian genre in Colombia and the roots of tango in the culture of the coffee-growing region.

Cover

Yezid Estarling Ciro Zapata (illustration).

Inner pages

· Kamyar Adl: p. 38 (photograph of kneeling man included in "Amansa Guapos" product image)—*Praying in Hamam (Bath House)*—© under Creative Commons license. [Online] available at: flickr.com/photos/kamshots/5741008074/.

· Jorge Andrés Cano Saldarriaga: pp. 28, 58-59.

· William Adolfo Cardona Bedoya: pp. 18-19, 34-35.

· Yezid Estarling Ciro Zapata: pp. 1, 38-39 (illustration and photocomposition).

· Hanner Steven Gómez Giraldo: p. 13 (right).

· Andrés Grajales: pp. 8-9, 10, 12, 16-17, 20-24, 26, 32-33, 36, 38-39 (only packaging and containers), 40-49, 54-57, 60-66, 68-71.

· Santiago Londoño González: pp. 7.

· Juan Sebastián López: p. 13 (left).

· Óscar López: p. 14.

· Lina Restrepo/Corporación Otraparte: pp. 50-51.

· Oscar Andrés Tobón Passos: pp. 30-31.

· Catalina Vásquez/Secretaría de Desarrollo Económico Alcaldía de Medellín: pp. 52-53.

· 'eatsmilesleep': p. 38 (photograph of casino roulette included in "Suerte Rápida" product image)—*roulette*—© under Creative Commons license. [Online] available at: flickr.com/photos/45378259@N05/6050121954/.

Gramatics Agencia Editorial expresses its gratitude to the people and institutions that, with the aim of promoting the culture of Medellín, have contributed in various ways with the preparation of this volume. We greatly appreciate the cooperation of:

· Adrissa S.A., in whose facilities some pictures were taken.
· Alberto Morales Peñalosa for his review of the historical background about tango in Medellín.
· Alianza Francesa Medellín, in whose facilities some photographs were taken.
· Ambroxia Beauty Salon Parque Lleras, whose professionals did the make-up and styling of artists in the fotograph of the article *Tango*.
· Área Metropolitana del Valle de Aburrá, especially Environmental Management officials Ana Cecilia Arbeláez Arboleda, Diana Fernanda Castro Henao, Eugenio Gaviria Cardona, Claudia Helena Hoyos Estrada and Ana Milena Joya Camacho, who provided technical information about the origin of the term *guayacán*, the characteristics of this species, its distribution, its cultivation, and its biological cycle.
· Asdrúbal Valencia Giraldo of the Academia Colombiana del Tango for his contribution regarding the past and present of the cultural offerings related to tango that exist in Medellín.
· Bar Boyacá, in whose facilities a photograph was taken for the article *Tango*.
· Carolina Buitrago Salazar for her support in some of the photo sessions.
· Corporación Otraparte for authorizing the use of the Casa Museo Otraparte photographs.
· Corporación de Silleteros de Santa Elena, especially Nelson Gaviria and Patricia Atehortúa Atehortúa, for their input regarding historical aspects of *silleteros* and the *Silleteros* Parade.

· El Candombe Academia de Baile for facilitating the use of image rights of the artist Jhon Alexánder Blandón.

· Elizabeth Vargas Jiménez, artisan and widow of the former president of the United Artisans Association of the Aburrá Valley, Jairo Sánchez Bustamante (1951-2014) who provided some information about the origin of the Sanalejo Market.

· Gloria Elena Erazo Garnica, a resident of Prado, for her contribution on the history and architectural characteristics of the Prado neighborhood.

· Hotel Nutibara, in whose facilities some pictures were taken.

· Jaime Jaramillo Panesso, who provided some of his literary and journalistic notes about the tango and the *carriel*.

· Joaquín Eduardo Álvarez Jiménez, who suggested bibliographical sources for the article *Tango*.

· Jorge Janna, in whose store Jorge Janna Arte Religioso the photographs for the article *Catholicism* were taken.

· Luis Fernando Marín Jaramillo from the division of Tourism Promotion of the Secretaría de Cultura Ciudadana de Medellín (Ministry of Citizen Culture of Medellín) for his guidance on historical information regarding the Mercado de Sanalejo.

· María Elvira Montoya, her sister Patricia, and her parents, who kindly welcomed us in their house to facilitate part of the photographic work.

· Plaza Mayor Medellín, in whose facilities some pictures were taken.

· Plaza Minorista José María Villa, where some pictures were taken.

· Restaurante Hato Viejo Las Palmas, where some pictures were taken.

· www.adelaidamejia.com for allowing us the use of image rights by artist Adelaida Mejía.